KT-424-510

CONTENTS

SUPERMAN
THE MAN OF STEEL

VITAL STATS

LIKES: A peaceful Metropolis
DISLIKES: Kryptonite
FRIENDS: Wonder Woman, Lois Lane
FOES: Lex Luthor
SKILLS: Heat vision
GEAR: Cape

SET NAMES: Superman (NYCC 2011 exclusive), Superman vs Power Armour Lex
SET NUMBERS: COMCON017, 6862
YEARS: 2011, 2012

A determined face: Superman is ready to stand for truth and justice.

Eye-catching red cape

DEFENDER OF METROPOLIS

On the other side of his double-sided face, Superman wears a confident smile – the Kryptonian enjoys banishing alien threats from his hometown, Metropolis.

Superman's yellow belt is also printed on his back.

The last survivor of the doomed planet Krypton, Superman was rocketed to Earth as a baby. Powered by the sun, the Man of Steel can fly faster than a speeding bullet, lift incredible weights and fire lasers from his eyes.

WONDER WOMAN
AMAZONIAN PRINCESS

VITAL STATS
....

LIKES: Honesty
DISLIKES: Lies
FRIENDS: Superman
FOES: Lex Luthor
SKILLS: Advanced fighting techniques
GEAR: Lasso of Truth

SET NAME: Superman vs Power Armour Lex
SET NUMBER: 6862
YEAR: 2012

The minifigure's hairpiece includes Wonder Woman's golden tiara.

Wonder Woman's costume is based upon the flag of the United States of America.

FORCING THE TRUTH
No one can lie once they're tangled in Wonder Woman's Lasso of Truth. A turn of her head shows how angry she was to be captured by Lex Luthor.

Born on Paradise Island, Amazonian Princess Diana trained to be a warrior from the moment she could fight. The strongest woman on the planet, she now fights crime as a member of the Justice League.

SHAZAM!
THE WORLD'S MIGHTIEST MORTAL

VITAL STATS

LIKES: Being a hero
DISLIKES: Being a kid
FRIENDS: The Justice League
FOES: Black Adam
SKILLS: Magical abilities
GEAR: White cape

SET NAME: Shazam
(SDCC 2012 exclusive)
SET NUMBER: COMCON020
YEAR: 2012

DID YOU KNOW?
Shazam appears in the LEGO® Batman™ 2: DC Comics Super Heroes and LEGO Batman 3: Beyond Gotham video games.

Shazam shares a hairpiece with Bruce Wayne

Printed body emblazoned with lightning strike

Shazam wears one of the longest capes to appear on a LEGO® DC Comics Super Heroes minifigure.

RAGE AND FURY
Shazam uses his great wisdom to think his way out of trouble. That doesn't means he always remains calm. The other side of Shazam's head shows him shouting in anger.

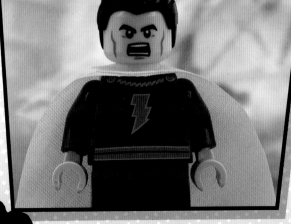

Aged ten, Billy Batson was granted magical powers by a wizard. By shouting "Shazam!" Billy changes into a powerful being blessed with the ability of legendary heroes Solomon, Hercules, Atlas, Zeus, Achilles and Mercury (spelling "Shazam").

JOR-EL
SUPERMAN'S FATHER

VITAL STATS
....

LIKES: Science
DISLIKES: The Kryptonian Council
FRIENDS: His wife Lara
FOES: General Zod
SKILLS: Code imprinting
GEAR: Dark brown cape

SET NAME: Jor-El (polybag)
SET NUMBER: 5001623
YEAR: 2013

DID YOU KNOW?
This minifigure is based on the 2013 *Man of Steel* movie. It was given free to customers at shop.LEGO.com and LEGO stores in June 2013.

Armour detailing is similar to Superman's *Man of Steel* variant

The "S" symbol means "hope" in Kryptonian.

FROM FATHER TO SON
As "Clark Kent", Superman discovered a Kryptonian spaceship on Earth. From it, a holographic image of Jor-El appeared to teach Clark about his alien heritage and present the Last Son of Krypton with his Superman uniform.

While Superman's armour is gold in tones, Jor-El's is bronze.

When chief scientist Jor-El realized that his planet Krypton was about to explode, he tried to warn the Kryptonian High Council. With Jor-El's advice going ignored, he sent his son to Earth for safety. This son would become Superman!

AQUAMAN
RULER OF ATLANTIS

VITAL STATS

LIKES: The ocean
DISLIKES: Ice prisons
FRIENDS: Batman
FOES: Mr Freeze
SKILLS: Controlling sea-life
GEAR: Golden trident

SET NAMES: Arctic Batman vs Mr Freeze: Aquaman on Ice, Black Manta Deep Sea Strike
SET NUMBERS: 76000, 76027
YEARS: 2013, 2015

An angry face as Aquaman plans a retaliation attack

Aquaman can blast water out of his trident.

Aquaman's muscles are also printed on the back of the minifigure.

FROZEN FISH

The marine minifigure's reversible head shows a more sombre expression. Aquaman had plenty of time to think when he was put on ice in Mr Freeze's petrifying polar prison.

Half–human and half–Atlantean, Aquaman tirelessly defends Earth's oceans from attack. The briny ruler is able to communicate telepathically with fish and sea mammals, and was one of the founding members of the Justice League.

GREEN ARROW
THE EMERALD ARCHER

VITAL STATS
••••••••••••••••••••

LIKES: Hitting the bull's-eye
DISLIKES: Commitment
FRIENDS: The Justice League
FOES: Merlyn
SKILLS: Archery
GEAR: Green hood

SET NAME: Green Arrow (SDCC 2013 exclusive)
SET NUMBER: COMCON030
YEAR: 2013

Green hood

DID YOU KNOW?
This is the only LEGO DC Comics Super Heroes Green Arrow minifigure not to have a bow and arrow!

Cool Super Hero stubble

Arrow insignia on belt

TWO'S COMPANY
This rare Green Arrow kept company with black-suited Superman at the 2013 San Diego Comic-Con.

Kneepads printed on legs

Another Comic-Con exclusive, 200 Green Arrow minifigures were offered up for raffle in July 2013. They are based on Green Arrow's updated 2011 costume from the comics. Previously, Green Arrow had sported a yellow goatee.

LOIS LANE
DAILY PLANET REPORTER

VITAL STATS
....

LIKES: Following leads
DISLIKES: Being kidnapped
FRIENDS: Superman
FOES: General Zod
SKILLS: Investigating,
escaping from aliens
GEAR: Wits and bravery

SET NAMES: Superman: Black
Zero escape
SET NUMBERS: 76009
YEARS: 2013

DID YOU KNOW?
This Lois Lane
minifigure is based on her
appearance in the 2013
Man of Steel movie.

Lois shares
her long red
hair with
eight other
minifigures.

Exclusive head
only available on
this minifigure

Printed blouse and
vest is suitable attire
for a newshound

ESCAPE POD PERIL
Is it any wonder the other side
of Lois' head has a terrified
expression? She's been thrown
out of General Zod's Black Zero
ship in an escape pod!

Practical blue
trousers

Intrepid reporter Lois Lane knew
she had a story on her hands from
the moment the first reports about
Superman came in. Following her
leads, she tracked the Man of Steel
to his Smallville home and
discovered his secret identity.

SUPERMAN
LAST SON OF KRYPTON

VITAL STATS

LIKES: Metropolis
DISLIKES: Falling structures
FRIENDS: Lois Lane,
Jimmy Olsen
FOES: General Zod
SKILLS: Heat vision
GEAR: Red cape

SET NAMES: Superman:
Metropolis Showdown,
Superman: Battle of
Smallville, Superman: Black
Zero Escape
SET NUMBERS: 76002,
76003, 76009
YEAR: 2013

Peek beneath the cape and
you'll see Superman's suit
also printed on the back of
the minifigure.

Silver armour
detailing, as befits
a battle-ready suit

Details of the suit
are also printed
on the legs.

PROPERTY OF TYDAL PUBLIC LIBRARIES

TURNING UP THE HEAT

One side of Superman's head
shows an angry expression and
red eyes as he fights to save
Metropolis and Smallville from
the villainous Zod. The other
side wears a calmer frown.

Darker than the classic Superman
outfit, this more modern-looking
Man of Steel has rid himself of the
red pants over his tights. This suit
is modelled on traditional Kryptonian
clothing, worn under battle armour
on Superman's home planet.

OFFROADER
BIG IN SMALLVILLE

DID YOU KNOW?
Brick-yellow pieces such as the Offroader's cabin, were first seen in the LEGO® Adventurers theme in 1998.

Flick-fire missiles

Rocket launcher can rotate by 360 degrees

Cabin with two seats is one piece

HARDY DEFENCE
Brave Colonel Hardy knows his Offroader's missile launcher is no match for General Zod's Black Zero Dropship, but he still uses it to defend Smallville when the Kryptonian criminal attacks.

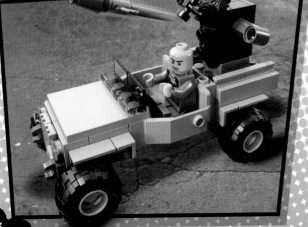

Chunky all-terrain tyres

This sand-coloured utility vehicle is equipped for battle, with searchlights and a pair of rocket launchers mounted on the back. It can seat two U.S. Air Force soldiers, and is driven by Colonel Hardy when the town of Smallville comes under attack.

COLONEL HARDY
U.S. AIR FORCE HERO

Bald head for this bold hero

Pockets to store ammo

Radio to call for back up

DID YOU KNOW?
Colonel Hardy shares a head with the Bank Guard from The Batmobile and the Two-Face Chase (set 8684).

GETTING THE DROP ON ZOD

Colonel Hardy becomes a hero when he stages an attack on Zod's spacecraft. He triggers a portal that drags the ship back to the Phantom Zone proving that the mighty Dropship is no match for the nifty offroader.

A member of the U.S. Air Force, Colonel Nathan Hardy was ordered to bring down the battling Kryptonians that were flattening Smallville. However, the Colonel realised that the Man of Steel wasn't their enemy after Superman saved his life.

THE FLASH
THE FASTEST MAN ALIVE

Remove the helmet
to find a two-sided
face complete with a
red mask surround.

Flip the head to
reveal an angry
expression

Exclusive
helmet with
yellow bolts
on each side

Costume printing
continues onto
the back of
the minifigure

Flash insignia

THE NEED FOR SPEED

The Flash was on hand to help
Batman chase down the Riddler's
dragster. With his acrobatic
abilities he jumps over the
Riddler's bombs (and bananas),
and remains in hot pursuit of
the questionable criminal.

DID YOU KNOW?

The Flash appears in
the LEGO *Batman 2: DC
Comics Super Heroes*
and LEGO *Batman 3:
Beyond Gotham*
video games.

After he was struck by lightning,
police scientist Barry Allen developed
the power to run at high speeds. Able
to outrun anything on the planet,
The Flash rushed into a life fighting
crime and was one of the founding
members of the Justice League.

SUPERBOY
THE BOY OF STEEL

VITAL STATS
....

LIKES: Being a hero
DISLIKES: Being called
Superboy
FRIENDS: Superman
FOES: Lex Luthor
SKILLS: Flight, Super-
strength
GEAR: Doesn't need any!

SET NAME: Minifigure
Gift Set
SET NUMBER: 5004076
YEAR: 2014

DID YOU KNOW?
Superboy's first LEGO
appearance was in
the videogame LEGO
*Batman 2: DC Super
Heroes*, where he wore
an all-black outfit.

Same tousled
hair as Robin

Muscle tone
shows through
tight shirt

Rare two-tone
minifigure arms
gives t-shirt
effect

A LIKELY LAD
In 2015 exclusive set 5004077
revealed another Super Hero
from faraway: Lightning Lad.
This character's ability to create
eletricity is shown with the
dramatic lightning bolts on his
minifigure's torso and legs.

Blue jeans show
Superboy's
casual approach
to costumes!

Conner Kent was cloned from Lex
Luthor and Superman's DNA, but
still became Superman's pal, earning
the Kryptonian name Kon-El. He has
similar abilities to Superman, such
as super strength, heat vision, x-ray
vision, freeze breath and flight.

GREEN LANTERN
GUARDIAN OF EARTH

VITAL STATS

LIKES: Protecting the Earth
DISLIKES: Losing his Lantern
FRIENDS: Batman
FOES: Sinestro
SKILLS: Space flight
GEAR: Green Lantern

SET NAME: Green Lantern
vs Sinestro
SET NUMBER: 76025
YEAR: 2015

Green Lantern shares
a hairpiece with
Commissioner Gordon.

A two-sided
head features
a grinning face
on the reverse

Green Lantern uniform
complete with the insignia
of the Lantern Corps

DOWN-TO-EARTH
An earlier Green Lantern, based
on the 2011 *Green Lantern*
movie, was given away to 1,500
raffle winners at the 2011 San
Diego Comic-Con, with a smaller
quantity released at New York
Comic Con the same year.

Black and green
printing continues
on the back

When test pilot Hal Jordan
discovered the wreckage of an alien
spacecraft he received a power ring
that transformed him into the Green
Lantern. Drawing power from his
cosmic lantern, Hal protects the
solar system from attack.

CONSTRUCT SPACESHIP
IMAGINE THAT!

DID YOU KNOW?
Green Lantern can use his power ring to make solid constructs of anything he imagines – not just spaceships!

Shooters on both wings

Forward shooters

A GIANT LEAP...
The Green Lantern vs Sinestro set also comes with a special Super Jumper piece that serves as a springboard for minifigures to perform giant leaps.

Made from energy channelled through a power ring, this spaceship only works while Green Lantern is concentrating! Hal Jordan creates it to chase after Sinestro, when the villain steals his Power Battery and takes it to the planet Korugar.

WONDER WOMAN
AMAZONIAN WARRIOR

Face printing appears in six other sets

Silver tiara

New battle-ready uniform exclusive to set

Trousers replace her satin tights

SWORD HELD HIGH
A twist of Wonder Woman's head reveals her scowling as she rushes into the fray, armed with her Amazonian sword. She's a foe to be reckoned with thanks to a lifetime of combat training.

Fighting crime in a modern age, the new Wonder Woman is based on an updated costume first introduced to the comics in 2011. Her armour is also printed on the back of her minifigure. Villains beware, this Wonder Woman is ready for battle.

INVISIBLE JET
NOTHING TO SEE HERE!

DID YOU KNOW?
Wonder Woman's
Invisible Jet can also
travel into outer
space – but only for
short periods
of time.

Hinged cockpit
canopy

Transparent
blue shooter

Missile
launcher
without
shooter

GORILLA TACTICS
Wonder Woman uses her
Invisible Jet to come to the
rescue of a Truck Driver in the
Gorilla Grodd Goes Bananas set.
The driver probably wishes he
was invisible, too!

Unique transparent
wing pieces

Wonder Woman built the
Invisible Jet in the name of peace.
By travelling unseen, she can carry
out her missions without starting
a fight. The plane is super-fast and
a complete stealth vehicle. Even
the exhaust flames are invisible!

TRUCK DRIVER
DRIVEN AROUND THE BEND

VITAL STATS
....

LIKES: Delivering fruit
DISLIKES: Angry customers, telepathic gorillas
FRIENDS: Batman, the Flash, Wonder Woman
FOES: Gorilla Grodd
SKILLS: Driving
GEAR: Bananas

SET NAME: Gorilla Grodd Goes Bananas
SET NUMBER: 76026
YEAR: 2015

Terrified expression

Back printing shows that this driver works for "Banana Co."

Happy banana logo

Practical dungarees

A BAD DAY AT WORK

First his truck is raided, then he's swung upside-down by a very hungry Grodd! It's shaping up to be a bad day for the truck driver. Frequent super-villain attacks mean there are lots of job vacancies in Gotham City as workers flee from danger.

Talk about being in the wrong place at the wrong time. All the Truck Driver had to do was deliver a batch of bright yellow bananas to Gotham City's fruit lovers. Easy – unless you run into a giant hyper-intelligent gorilla.

GREEN ARROW
ANGRY ARCHER

VITAL STATS
....

LIKES: Shooting straight
DISLIKES: A close shave
FRIENDS: Superman, Cyborg
FOES: Darkseid
SKILLS: Archery
GEAR: Longbow

SET NAMES: Darkseid
Invasion
SET NUMBERS: 76028
YEARS: 2015

Face stubble
printing reveals
that the Green
Archer is in need
of a shave

Green plastic
hood hangs
from around
the neck

ARMED AND DANGEROUS

You can swivel the Green
Arrow's head to reveal an angry
expression. A quiver full of
arrows is also printed on the
back of his torso, beneath
his cape.

Standard LEGO
bow and arrow
in green

With a body similar to the earlier
San Diego Comic-Con exclusive,
this Green Arrow has plain green
legs rather than kneepads. Luckily
for the Justice League, the Arrow
stays on target no matter what his
workday wardrobe.

THE JAVELIN
THE JUSTIC LEAGUE'S SPACESHIP

VITAL STATS

OWNER: Green Arrow
USED FOR: Justice League missions
GEAR: Bombs, rockets

SET NAMES: Darkseid Invasion
SET NUMBERS: 76028
YEARS: 2015

Double doors open to reveal large cargo bay

DID YOU KNOW?
Darkseid Invasion was the first set to include a springy Super Jumper element – hidden in the Javelin's cargo bay.

Justice League emblem on nose cone

A lever can tilt the wing tips upwards for landing.

There is room inside the cockpit for Green Arrow's bow alongside the archer.

JAW-DROPPING
The underside of the Javelin has two rocket launchers and a bomb door that opens like a jaw to drop its cargo – or to scoop up an enemy minifigure!

Green Arrow flies this sleek Justice League jet, which can travel through air, underwater, or in the vacuum of space. It was built by Batman and is equipped with all the gadgets and gear you'd expect from him – just not in his usual dark colour scheme!

HAWKMAN
WINGED WARRIOR

Golden helmet also winged to be aerodynamic

VITAL STATS

LIKES: Flying high
DISLIKES: Having his wings clipped
FRIENDS: Superman, Cyborg, Green Arrow
FOES: Darkseid
SKILLS: Flight
GEAR: Wings, Mace

SET NAMES: Darkseid Invasion
SET NUMBERS: 76028
YEARS: 2015

Wings attach to Hawkman's minifigure using gold studs.

BEATING WINGS

Hawkman comes with two interchangeable set of plastic wings, one spread out for flight and the other drawn in for fight! There's also a two-sided head beneath that helmet.

Hawk symbol joins crossing chest straps

Archaeologist Carter Hall uses magical Nth Metal to soar through the air as the savage Hawkman. This Justice League member is no young featherweight – he's actually a reincarnated Egyptian prince!

Project Editor Emma Grange
Editors Tina Jindal, Matt Jones, Ellie Barton,
Clare Millar, Rosie Peet
Senior Designers Nathan Martin, Mark Penfound,
David McDonald
Designers Karan Chaudhary, Stefan Georgiou
Pre-Production Producer Kavita Varma
Senior Producer Lloyd Robertson
Managing Editors Paula Regan,
Chitra Subramanyam
Design Managers Neha Ahuja, Guy Harvey
Creative Manager Sarah Harland
Art Director Lisa Lanzarini
Publisher Julie Ferris
Publishing Director Simon Beecroft

Additional Photography Markos Chouris,
Christopher Chouris, Gary Ombler

First published in Great Britain in 2016
by Dorling Kindersley Limited
80 Strand, London, WC2R 0RL

001–298875–Jul/16

Contains content previously published in LEGO® DC COMICS
SUPER HEROES *Character Encyclopedia* (2016)

Page design copyright © 2016 Dorling Kindersley Limited
A Penguin Random House Company

LEGO, the LEGO logo, the Brick and Knob configurations
and the Minifigure are trademarks of the LEGO Group.
© 2016 The LEGO Group. All rights reserved.
Manufactured by Dorling Kindersley
under licence from the LEGO Group.

A CIP catalogue record for this book
is available from the British Library.

ISBN: 978-0-2412-9288-4

Printed and bound in China

www.LEGO.com
www.dk.com

ACKNOWLEDGEMENTS
DK would like to thank Randi Sørensen,
Paul Hansford, Martin Leighton Lindhardt, Maria
Bloksgaard Markussen, Adam Corbally, Daniel
Mckenna, Casper Glahder, Adam Siegmund Grabowski,
John Cuppage, Justin Ramsden, Karl Oskar Jonas
Norlen, Marcos Bessa, Sally Aston, Sven Robin Kahl
and Mauricio Bedolla at the LEGO Group; Ben Harper,
Thomas Zellers and Melanie Swartz at Warner Bros.;
Cavan Scott and Simon Hugo for their writing
and Sam Bartlett for design assistance.

A WORLD OF IDEAS:
SEE ALL THERE IS TO KNOW